The Future Wife Handbook:

You're Not Waiting, You're Preparing

Lessons every future wife should know.

ACE METAPHOR

ISBN-10: 1548161918
ISBN-13: 978-1548161910

DEDICATION

To my mother, I love you.

To my father, I look up to you.

To my Metaphorically Speaking family, this wouldn't have been possible without you.

To my online supporters, you give me purpose – for that I am grateful.

Thank you for believing in me.

Connect with me on social media:

Facebook.com/acemetaphor

Instagram.com/acemetaphor

Send a picture of yourself holding the book to
acemetaphorpoetry@gmail.com.

Be sure to include your social media handle.

Be creative, you may be featured on one of my social media pages.

Love to you all.

LET ME TALK TO YOU

Look, I'm just an ordinary guy who lives in an ordinary city and has an ordinary job. And it's that ordinary life that's shown me something about people – we know what to do, but we don't do it. Or we know, but we don't know that we know.

That's especially true in our relationships, our lives, our dating world.

And that is the reason I wrote this book. It's a reminder for us all. As we go about our ordinary lives, we need to stop thinking about waiting for our future spouses, we need to prepare for love that lasts a lifetime by loving ourselves first.

Think about it – we say, "To have and to hold," during our wedding ceremonies, but when do we say that to ourselves? When do we commit to loving ourselves?

I believe that you can't love somebody else 'til you've learned to love yourself first. You can't give what you don't have.

See, I think we've been taught to love wrong. We should say our vows to ourselves first. We look into the eyes of our partner and whisper sweet nothings, but we don't look into the mirror and say the same things to ourselves.

At this moment, whether you're single, in a relationship, or are about to be single again, you want things to get better. Even if things are great right now, you want them to get better.

That's why I wrote this book. Each chapter is a quick and easy read for you to digest on the go or before bed.

The fact is, wherever you're at, you shouldn't be waiting for someone else to love you. Because you can give yourself all the love you need right now.

Only once you're prepared to love yourself unconditionally is it time to go find love from someone else.

So as you read what's been on my mind and heart these past few years, I want you to love yourself. Commit to yourself.

Then maybe, just maybe, we'll all have our happily ever after's. You're not waiting, you're preparing.

ACE METAPHOR

BEFORE YOU LET SOMEONE

Before you let a man sweep you off your feet, be sure he is prepared to catch you when you fall. You might be too much woman for him. You might be too independent, too smart, too much of a catch. He may not be ready for the weight of how beautiful you are, how gorgeous you are, how strong you are. He may not be ready yet. You have to be prepared to be yourself whether he can carry you or not.

Before you let someone sweep you off your feet, be sure he is strong enough, secure enough in himself. Be sure he has the proper amount of self-esteem, self-confidence to handle how awesome you are.

For men, it's important for you to know their past, their attributes, their strengths, their weaknesses, if he's prepared to handle how beautiful you are, how gorgeous, how so awesome you are.

I'm here to tell you that it's super important to take your time. Don't just listen to sweet nothings. Words can be lies. Watch actions because your heart is too precious to be mishandled by a player or a temptress. Your brain doesn't need a bruise from the one you thought loved you.

YOUR CROWN

Most people think it's easy to be you, that it's easy to be royalty. But I know it's hard. I know it's difficult to maintain your morals and your standards in this world. While you're out there handling yourself with class, dignity, and respect, there are women who take shortcuts to get the man. They're not working as hard, they're not holding to their morals and values. Now, every man you meet expects you to be like them. They look at you like you're crazy when you tell them that you've got morals and standards that you're not willing to compromise. Their negative responses make you wonder if this queen isn't the best way to go about it.

If you feeling that way, don't let the haters get to you. Don't compromise. Don't give up your crown simply because you can't find a man who has the integrity to hold it yet. Don't start thinking that you've gotta be like other women, that you've gotta start having sex sooner than you want to, that you've gotta submit to somebody who doesn't deserve your respect.

You need to find your king, the one for you.

Why does everybody in this world think it's easy to be a queen? I know how hard it is, so that makes me appreciate you more.

Keep doing you because your king will see you. And when he does, there will be no doubt who you are – his queen.

YOU ARE WORTH IT

You are worth every flower.

You are worth every date.

You are worth every minute, hour, second, week, year ... whatever the wait, you are worth it.

You are worth every compliment.

You are worth every moon, every sun – those that science has found and those it hasn't. You are worth the stars, the universe, the galaxy. You are worth everything. You are worth all the attention, every effort, and every moment of time spent.

You are worth anything and everything it takes to earn you. And quit letting anybody convince you otherwise. Quit letting the world's standards dictate yours. Don't lower your standards for what you expect from a man. Don't expect less just so more people can qualify for the position of holding your heart.

Your heart is worth the wait, too. Wait until you find the man that's going to give anything and everything, a man that deserves you.

'Cause you are worth it.

MAN OR NOT

You are enough for you.

You are enough for you.

Quit letting people make you think you need somebody else to complete you, or to make you better, or to make you happy.

You have special gifts that God gave you at birth – your heart and your mind. Those are the only ingredients you need to keep yourself happy. Just look inside yourself for validation, not other people.

We say, "She's my other half. He's my better half. Now I'm complete."

But our completion starts within ourselves, by looking inside ourselves.

I don't care what Disney tells you; your "happily ever after" doesn't start with a man. Your happily ever after begins when you look inside your own heart and realize that, regardless of who is in your corner or not, you are a queen – and forever will be.

Man or no man, you're a queen. So act like it.

SAVING HIS PLACE

Have you ever been out somewhere saving a seat, and somebody walks past you and says, "Hey, anybody sitting right there?"

Then you say, "Yeah, I'm saving this seat for my girl. They're just getting drinks. Be right back."

Then what do they say?

"I was just asking because you look lonely. I can keep you company."

And you shut them down.

"No, I'm saving this seat for the person that's supposed to be in that seat."

The same thing should happen when you are sleeping alone. Just because somebody isn't right next to you doesn't mean you are alone.

You're just saving that seat for your man, for your woman – for that right person who will come along at the right time.

You're not going to lay next to just anybody. You're saving that place for the right person at the right time in the right circumstances in your life and you aren't going to compromise. You're not alone just because you sleep alone.

Don't let loneliness make you occupy your bed with the wrong type of person, because if you do, there won't be a space for the right person at the right time at the right point in your life.

"This seat is taken."

IT'S OKAY TO BE SINGLE

Whenever someone tries to make you feel bad for not having a man, tell them, "Talk to the hand, 'cause the brain ain't listening!" These, my friend, are misguided haters. They want to tie your womanhood to your ability to keep a man or not.

They don't understand. You've got a plan, and you're sticking to it. You can get any man you want, any woman you want, and they don't understand that fact. You can literally walk out there and pick a guy off the street and he'll have you tonight if he could. You can probably take your pick of the 20 or 30 men in your inbox right now.

And you could be sort of happy with them, but you don't want a man; you want your man.

Understand something about yourself. You choosing right now to be disciplined enough to not pick just any person and instead wait for yours doesn't make you less of a woman. It actually makes you more of one, a more disciplined, more attractive version of yourself. So if the haters don't understand that, tell them, "Talk to the hand, cause the brain ain't listening."

NOT WAITING BUT PREPARING

You wait for nobody. You need nobody to save you. You were equipped with a crown at birth, so you are royalty by nature, whether or not you have a king yet.

But you don't have to wait, because waiting is a passive thing. You hope and pray something happens to you because you need it, you're desperate for it.

The truth is, you don't need somebody to be happy. You don't need somebody to be complete. You are already given all the puzzle pieces, you just have to figure out how to put them together before you meet that person. So waiting does nothing. It's a passive action.

I need you to actively prepare for the love of your life by loving the love of your life, which is yourself. Love you with your whole heart, your whole mind, and your whole soul. You've gotta love you cause you're gonna wake up every day to you. You're gonna see yourself in the mirror every day.

So every day you have to love you. You have to grow that love. You have to practice with yourself, so one day, you can love somebody just as much for the rest of theirs, so you ain't waiting. You're preparing.

DO SOMETHING

Thinking about giving up on love?
Don't.
Don't give up on love. You're just sitting on that couch right now with nothing to do. If there's anything you shouldn't do, it's that.
Prepare your heart. Get up and study. Learn how to be a better you, for yourself and for a better person. Learn how to do all those things you wish a person would do for you.
You don't have anything else to do. You could be going to college, learning about yourself, mastering practical skills.
Sometimes you can get so disheartened that you give up, and that's the worst thing to do right now. Never give up. Never stop trying. Never stop thinking that there is not a good man out there, because there is. The right person is waiting for you, but you will never cross paths if you are sitting there on that couch doing nothing, playing on your phone.
So get up and get your heart ready to love again.

LOVE YOU FOR YOU

Listen, I don't care how big you are, how small you are, how tall you are, what shade, what color, whatever. The man that decides to love you should love every inch, every shade, every follicle, every molecule of you. Period. Not open to discussion, all right?

Let me tell you what's going to happen. When you start to believe what you just read, you will come across people in this world who tell you how unrealistic all that is. The idea of love has been misconstrued so much that it's now considered unrealistic for a person to love you just the way you are.

The haters are going want you to believe that, but I want you to tell them, "No!" Because there is somebody out there that who will love every fiber of you. Every little bit that you have inside you. And they are going to love you just the way you are. They won't hope you change, want you to change, or expect you to change unless it's already your desire to change for the better, unless you want to graduate to another level in life.

No matter what, love you first, unconditionally. Then let somebody else love whatever you have to offer. That's not unrealistic. It's only keeping it real.

LOVE YOU DESPITE WHAT OTHERS THINK

Do you remember that person you were so madly in love with despite your family and friends not liking them?

Nobody you knew liked them, not your cousin Pookey or your dog Spot. It didn't matter, did it? Because you were in love with them. Nobody's opinions mattered, they didn't faze you. You two were together. You didn't care what anybody thought, but at the same time, and for whatever reason, you allow those same haters' opinions to affect how you view yourself. Think about that. Your friends, your family, people on social media, you let them all affect how much you love yourself. I challenge you to start loving yourself like you love that partner nobody accepted. Despite what other people think, love yourself just the way you are. Love yourself unconditionally.

MINGLE

The last time I checked, nobody is hand-delivering 50 or 60 years of a perfect relationship to anybody's doorstep.

So maybe, just maybe, you're gonna have to get out that bed, put some clothes on, get dressed, and go mix and mingle with high quality people.

Maybe, just maybe, your Prince Charming has spent his whole life looking for you, but he hasn't found you yet, because you're sitting at home alone. He is looking high and low, under every rock, on top of every mountain, but that doesn't do any good because you're on top of your mattress right now watching Netflix.

Look, I know it's difficult. I know it's tough. You're probably a "home body" like me, but in order to be found, you've gotta be where people are looking.

Maybe he's looking for you.

Maybe he can't find you 'cause you're in the house watching Netflix just like me.

Let's turn the TV off and get back out there.

DATE MYSELF

I'm going to take myself out on a nice date, by myself. Nobody else there. I'm going to order some chicken, some waffles, some wine. I'm going to sit and talk to myself. I'm going to ask, "Self, how was your day?" Me and myself, we're going to converse. We're going to talk about everything in life that we need to discuss.

We're going to have that "me" time. We're going to have that meditation time. We're going to have that figuring out life time. Then we're going to talk about our perfect day, and I'm going to date myself. I'm going to get to know myself. I'm going to treat myself right. And I'm going to buy myself flowers.

I don't need anybody to wine and dine me, because I can do that myself. I don't need anybody to make me happy, because I can do that myself. I don't even need anybody to converse with, because I can do that myself.

So when a potential partner comes along, they'd better know how to behave. Because I'm used to treating myself well, I'll be damned if I let somebody treat me badly just because they aren't living up to the standards I'm holding myself to.

MAKE HER FEEL SPECIAL

When you like her – when you really, really like her – you need to text her, "Good morning."

Just because. Just because you want her to know that she's the first thing on your mind when you wake up.

Then buy her flowers. Take her on walks. Take her out on real dates. Show her some scenery. Tell her how beautiful she is. Do all of that for her because you want her to feel special. Not all the "hers", just her. When you put in all of that for every "her" you meet, that doesn't make her feel special anymore.

It's only special when you do it for her. When you complement her, it matters that you don't think everybody is pretty. Just her.

When you're pulling out her chair, opening her doors, and staying faithful to her, all of it makes her feel special. But she doesn't feel special if you're doing that for every single person you meet.

So be a gentleman to her. Be faithful to her. Gain her trust. Tell her she's beautiful. Make her feel special.

SERVE HER

Before you tell her you love her, get ready to serve her.

Do you understand what love means? Commitment that requires a lot from you. Do understand that when you say, "I love you," that requires you to be in a servant position, ready to protect her.

No matter how difficult or impossible the odds may seem, that is your job now, to protect her. Are you ready to do that?

Before you tell her you love her, are you ready to provide for her?

No matter what it takes to keep a meal on that table for her and the offspring you two are gonna have together, are you ready to build her up mentally? Are you ready to be there for her spiritually?

I know you love her, but are you ready to serve her? Are you ready to work for her? Are you ready to give hours and hours of your time to make sure she becomes a better person? Are you ready to be her teammate?

That's what I want to know. I know you love her, but are you ready to take care of her? Are you ready to serve her?

PHONE CALL

The most overlooked, underappreciated quality in a person is the ability to pick up the phone when you call.

When you're going through something and you call somebody, you hope it only rings twice, maybe three times, and they pick up the phone. You know you can count on them to be there for you.

But then there's the person who lets it go to voicemail 5 times out of 8. Then when they do finally respond by texting you, it's obvious they didn't even listen to your voicemail because they say, "Hey, you called?"

"Yeah, I called because I needed to talk to you. I didn't want to text."

Why don't some people understand that? I think we've lost the art of communicating with each other effectively. Some days, you just wanna talk to somebody, not just text.

Why do we have to text all the time? Why can't we communicate? Why can't I hear your voice?

Maybe I just want to hear how your voice sounds. I can't do that with just letters. Maybe I've got something important I want to tell you, and I don't want to do it through text.

The most overlooked quality in this life is being capable of picking up the phone when you call, and talking to you like a real person.

MAKE A LIST

I'm making a list, and I'm checking it twice.

What about you?

Are you making a list of everything you need from a mate? Everything you want from your potential lover who you're with for the rest of your life?

Do you make a list of those 10 things you absolutely have to have? And there's no wavering from those 10 things because without them, you won't be happy.

Is that what you're doing? Or do you meet somebody and think, "That person is cute." Then you start scratching things off the list. You start compromising on what you actually want.

Before you met that person, you made your list. You thought it through. You planned to accept into your life only what is best for you. So then why do you let your feelings take over and cross things off that list? You get impatient and start crossing things off that list so more people can meet your criteria. Why?

Are you making a list and checking it twice every time you meet somebody? That's what you should be doing. Never cross anything out. If they're the right person for you, you won't ever be tempted to cross anything off that list. Because they'll meet every single thing you're looking for.

MEANT TO BE

True love is me thinking about you thinking about me thinking about you – for every day of our lives. Before we even meet, there have to be pieces of ourselves in each other already.

When we meet, it isn't going to be as difficult as chemistry class.

We will look at each other and say together, "Oh, this is meant to be. This is us!"

When two people are meant to be together, there is no need to force things. You two are made for each other. It's a perfect fit, and it just seems right.

So the laughs flow. The jokes flow. The conversations flow. You are willing to compromise, they're willing to compromise.

Don't let the world convince you that love is supposed to be hard, because it should be easy when you're with the right person.

Maybe it's hard right now because you're not with that right person. Maybe you're crying, you're hurt, you're lonely right now.. But one day, when you find the right person, they will have pieces of you inside of them already. And you will be inside of them.

PREPARE FOR THE TRIP

Not everything that should work out, does.

Good relationships fail, just like a perfectly planned trip fails. If somebody doesn't pack the right gear for the trip, things won't go well. Have you ever decided to take a trip around the world or were gone for a week or two or went on a cruise, and you didn't pack everything you needed? You left your flat iron at the crib, your left that sexy pair of heels behind, your deodorant stick, whatever. So now, you have to go the whole cruise looking, feeling, or smelling bad because you didn't pack. You didn't prepare well. You didn't check everything off that checklist like you should have.

It's the same in relationships. You've gotta prepare your heart adequately for the length and the duration of your relationship. Did you pack your briefcase with endurance? Did you pack it with patience? Did you pack it with problem-solving skills?

These are just a few things you need for a long-term relationship. Now, if you just want a weekend fling, you don't need that. You can just pick something up at the mall. But if you want something that will last for a while, it's your job to prepare. Sometimes it's not the relationship that's bad – it's your preparation skills.

CREDIT SCORES

Even if I can like you in this present moment, there's something you need to know.

Before I give my heart to you, before I lend you my heart, I'm gonna check your relationship credit score.

Your character credit score.

Your past credit score.

I'm checking all three . Even as I'm writing this I hear the haters.

"Well, that's in the past! It don't matter, it's in the past!"

You're right, it is in the past. But those past mistakes, past experience, and past moves let me know who you are now, how far you've come, if you've made progress, and what you will most likely do in the future. Before I give you something important like my heart, I need to know.

If we're gonna be life partners, isn't it important for me to know if you've defaulted on relationships before? If you've committed fraud and aren't the person you claim to be? If you're overdue on giving love when somebody needed it most?

I ain't saying you've gotta be perfect. But I am saying that your score had better be at least 672 before you'll find yourself in a relationship with me.

WINTER TIME

I'm sick of people who want to love for just tonight and not for forever. When are we going to see the bigger picture?

People out there tell me, "Winter time is coming. For now, you've gotta get you a cuddle buddy!"

"Winter time is coming"?

What about a lifetime cuddle buddy? That's what I want.

Anybody can be there for you for one night. Anybody. But only a few can last a lifetime. The problem is, if you keep occupying your time with tonight people, you'll lose sight of the forever people. See the bigger picture. Yes, I know you want to be loved right now, and right now is important. But there's somebody out there who will love you now and forever.

Yes, I need somebody to keep me warm this winter, but if there's no intention stay through spring and beyond, then I'd rather stay cold.

LET THEM LOVE YOU

Sometimes it's easier to love somebody with your whole heart, your whole mind, and your whole soul 'til death do you part, than it is to let them love you in the same way.

Sometimes we're scared. When we find something amazing out there, we get scared. When we finally get what we we're hoping for, it's hard to believe it's true. There are so many people out there who are wrong for us that it can be hard to accept somebody who is right for us!

When everything is going good, we start to wonder, "Hell, it's too good. It's too right. It's too perfect."

That's what we believe now, that it would be too good to be true to find somebody perfect for you. So, you start planting seeds of doubt in your relationship.

Don't do it. If it's right, let it be. If they love you, let them love you – with their whole heart. Quit getting in the way of that.

FALL IN LOVE WITH ME

People out here are building relationships based entirely on how somebody looks, as if that's going to sustain a relationship for 50 to 60 years. What's tight and firm now becomes saggy and flabby in just a few short years, ain't no way to stop that! Looks depreciate with time, and people don't realize that.

You can't fall in love with my looks. This is my vessel, this is my body, but it's not me. Me is inside. My spirit, my soul. It's what moves my body. Fall in love with my spirit. Fall in love with my soul. That doesn't depreciate with time.

Just like I build my body up, I build my mind up, and this won't work unless you realize what the real prize is. I realize that inside your cranium is who you really are, and if we want to make it to 50 or 60 years, we can't build our foundation based off of how each other looks, because it'll never work. Bodies always crumble. So will yours. But my mind will last forever. Fall in love with it, and we can see our 50 or 60 years.

SICK OF THE SINGLE LIFE

"I'm sick of this single life. I'm tired of going out to the clubs. I'm tired of being lonely. I'm ready to settle down."

What? Settling down doesn't have anything to do with you being sick of the club or feeling lonely. What does that even mean, being ready to settle down? I'll tell you – it means being ready for a relationship, that you have your life in order.

You know where you want to go in life. You have yours goals, and you're gonna meet them. And you have the proper tools to sustain a relationship.

Just because you're tired of shaking that ass doesn't mean you're ready to show your ass in a relationship.

So if you're tired of going to the club, stop going to the club. If you're lonely, get a dog or a Netflix password. But don't think for a minute that you're ready to be in a fruitful, productive relationship. That takes two grownups who are both ready to commit, both ready to love somebody with all of their hearts. Just being bored and sick of something won't cut it.

SHOPPING FOR LOVE HUNGRY

Have you ever gone to the grocery store, and you were mad hungry? You only went there for two items, but you left with a whole cart of shit you didn't even want in the first place.

That's exactly what just happened to me. I headed to the grocery for a Snickers bar, but I left with pineapples, pears, oatmeal, protein shakes, and yogurt.

I even bought some frozen vegetables and fresh vegetables that I'm pretty sure I'm not even gonna eat it. They're probably gonna sit in my refrigerator for a couple of weeks and spoil.

That's what happens when you shop hungry.

And that's the same thing that happens when you go shopping for love and you're lonely. The same exact thing – you end up with a bunch of stuff you didn't really want.

When you go shopping for love when you're lonely, you compromise your morals. You end up over-giving, overpaying. You end up grabbing the first thing you see, because you wanna satisfy that loneliness.

So my advice is, satisfy your loneliness before you go looking for a relationship. That way, you won't compromise and end up with stuff you don't need and you don't want.

Don't let your heart spoil.

IF YOU'RE NOT READY

If you're not ready for a relationship, stay in the house. Lock it. Turn on Netflix and try your best not to break somebody's heart. That's a full-time job nowadays. You not being ready for a relationship is your signal to not to get into one! I don't care how lonely, sick, and tired of the clubs you are. Feeling like you're done with the single life doesn't mean you're ready for a relationship.

I don't care how much you're ready to love somebody. Being ready to love somebody and being able to give fruitfully and wholeheartedly and purposefully to a relationship are two different things.

So right now while you're single, do everything. Go to Mt. Everest. Get a pedicure, manicure. Take a vacation. Work to get your college degree. Do whatever you've gotta do to make sure that you are a full person before you meet somebody.

If you're not ready for a relationship, don't get into one. It's harder to put that heart back together than it is to avoid breaking it in the first place.

TREAT YOU

When people say, "Treat others the way you want to be treated," we take that to mean we should expect others to do that – to treat us the way we want to be treated.

No, that's not how it works. People aren't gonna automatically treat you the way they want to be treated. If they don't have a standard or hold themselves to certain values, morals, or ethics.

They can't treat you well if that's the case, so you treating them well doesn't build your relationship karma. You treating yourself well, does.

When you treat you the way you want to be treated, that shows other people the standard you hold yourself to, and it lets them know that in order to get into your life, they've gotta meet that standard, especially when it comes to dating.

If you are treating yourself well and showing that you love yourself, that forces anybody who wants to be in your life to step their game up.

In other words, I want you to stop treating others the way you want to be treated and expecting them to do the same for you. It's unrealistic, and it doesn't happen. Sorry.

VERBAL CONTRACT

If you tell me that you love me, understand that you are signing a verbal contract. You are making a verbal contract with me. It's a big deal.

Before you say those words, be sure you are ready to honor, love, and respect me. Don't just say those words loosely, 'cause they mean something special to me. Those words mean everything to me.

I want you to understand what they mean – because saying them brings with those words a responsibility on your shoulders to show that you love me.

I know what that responsibility means, so when I say, "I love you" back, I know that means I've gotta take care of you. I've gotta be there for you. I've gotta promise to never hurt you and do the basic, fundamental things that a boyfriend or a girlfriend should do.

I know you think you love me, so I'm just asking you to be sure before you say it. It comes with expectations when you say those three powerful words.

SIZE OF HIS HEART

Sadly, there are many people out there who care more about the size of the ring on your finger than the size of your man's heart. Then we wonder why divorce rates are so high, and marriages are failing.

Because most people put more emphasis on the wedding than what happens after the wedding, as if getting married is the end of your journey! It's not.

People get comfortable after they marry. They think they've won, so they can coast for the next 50 to 60 years.

No. It takes work. But are you putting in that work before you get married? The same amount of work you're putting in to what colors you're going to have, the dress you're going to wear, how your hair looks, what your bridesmaids will do?

You've been thinking about that day since you were a little kid. You have to put in equal effort to what happens after the wedding. How are you going to sustain this relationship?

Anybody can get married; two become one. But not everybody can continue to maintain growing as one. You've got to put emphasis on knowing what's going to happen after you get married – not just what you're going to eat at your wedding.

HOLD ON WHEN IT'S RIGHT

When you find the right person for you – that person who gives you their whole heart, their whole mind, and their whole soul unconditionally – don't play games.

We live in a world today where too many bad people are dressed like good people.

Too many people are pretending to give something. When you undress the layers of their soul, and you find that they are who they say they are, and they want to make you happy every time you wake up, love them. Really love them.

Pull out chairs. Go on dates. Make them smile. Send "good morning" texts. Send them flowers. Write them notes.

Think about it. How much is your smile worth? How much is your happiness worth? How much is being with a faithful partner worth?

It's worth the extra effort, so when you find somebody who is for you exclusively, who loves every bit of you, then love every bit of them back.

There aren't too many people like that anymore.

OTHER 3%

Maybe we're not supposed to find our other half.
Maybe they're not supposed to be 50% of us.
Maybe they're supposed to be only 3%. Maybe before we meet them, we've gotta be 97% complete, and the only way we can be fully complete is by finding that other 3%.
But you've gotta be 97% of you, 97% happy, 97% self-sufficient. You've gotta maintain your independence. You've gotta be confident that you are enough for you.
But we don't do that. We overly rely on the wrong people at the wrong time to give us the boost we should have within ourselves.
I want my completion, but I don't need 50%, just 3%.
Give me that 3%.

ONLY SOURCE OF HAPPINESS

It is possible for somebody to make you happy in the moment, or even to provide momentary moments of happiness over the years ahead.

But it is almost impossible for them to be your only source of happiness.

Too often, we look for other people to fill the void we have inside, and then we think that there's no one good enough for us, that there's no one who fits us. But the fact is, we don't fit ourselves. That's the problem. You have to start making yourself happy. You have to be your own personal source of sunshine.

No one will ever be enough to complete you if you're not already complete yourself.

SHOW ME YOUR TIME

I'm sick.

Sick of people.

Sick of people telling me how much they care about me to gauge whether or not they really do.

Because words can be deceiving. What really tells you about a person is where they spend their time and on what.

We are all given 24 hours in a day. Where people spend those hours tells you everything you need to know about them...and everything about how they feel about you. Because if somebody truly desires to win your heart, they will spend the proportional amount of time doing it. But if 23 hours goes to work and you get the leftover scraps, you know that person wants to be successful at work, not at a relationship with you.

So from this moment on, when your special somebody makes you feel less than special, straight up tell them, "Listen, I know you say that you care about me, but where your time is being spent, proves whether or not that's true. So I don't need you to tell me you care about me if you don't spend the time proving that you do. If you care about me, your time will be here, not there. So don't tell me. Show me with your time."

ROUTINE MAINTENANCE

You can't ride your relationship until the wheels fall off, thinking that will get you to paradise.

You can't wait until your engine is about to blow then decide, "Dang, maybe I need to go to a mechanic." It takes routine maintenance and regular tune-up's on your relationship to make it work...and keep on working.

Are you scheduling that maintenance? Are you checking in every three months, every six months, to see what that other person wants? It's worth it to check in and see if this relationship is going in a direction that makes them happy, and vice versa for you.

You can't wait until problems and complaints add up into a massive blowup where you scream at each other, "I need you to work on this and this and this!"

Don't let your car break down like that. Take your relationship to the mechanic often.

Whenever a problem arises, solve it. If you don't do that with your car, why would you do that to your relationship?

Routine maintenance. Fix problems. Diagnostics. That's how you make it to paradise with your significant other.

Ready for a road trip?

YOU NEED GAS

It's the oldest excuse in the book. And it's the worst.
"But I love him! But I love her!"
As if love was enough to sustain a relationship.
Hold on, isn't it supposed to be?
I don't think so. If you're trying to go forward in a relationship, love is like your car. You absolutely need it. It's the thing most people see when they look at your relationship to know if it's healthy or not.

But just because you love somebody doesn't mean you communicate well. Just because you love somebody don't mean you trust them. Just because you love somebody don't mean that person is faithful to you.

Think about your car again. What good is it to have a shiny new million-dollar vehicle if you don't have the gas to sustain it for the journey? You might as well not even set off on that trip.

If you want your relationship to sit in the parking lot and look pretty, then maybe you don't need trust. Maybe you don't need faithfulness. Maybe you don't need loyalty. Maybe you do need any gas to go anywhere.

So if you want love, I need trust, communication, and problem-solving skills.

Because love itself isn't enough.

NO PERFECT RELATIONSHIP

There's no such thing as a perfect relationship. There are people who could be perfect for you, but in essence, you and your partner are both imperfect.

A relationship is the joining of two imperfect people, so problems are gonna come up. There will be situations, difficult things you've gotta deal with.

I wish I could tell you that there is a "get out of jail free" card or an "easy button" or an MJ secret sauce to this relationship thing.

But honestly, the best advice I can give is this: Be willing to get dirty. Be willing to roll up your sleeves, put the elbow grease in, and get to work on your relationship. There are no quick fixes, and it's gonna take time.

It's gonna take energy. It's gonna take effort. Sometimes, you're gonna feel tired afterward because it was strenuous work. But you've gotta work for your relationship to work.

So roll up those sleeves, and get to work.

STILL SAY IT

So many times in life we dismiss words because we think our actions are all that matters.

Yes, action is 90% of the work of love. "Love," is an action word, which means that when I say, "I love you," I have to act in harmony with that.

Most often, a person will know that you love them by your actions. When you open doors, when you go the extra mile, when you are attentive, caring, and respectful. When you buy gifts and remember birthdays. All of these tell that special person that they're special to you – you didn't have to say a word.

But just because you can show somebody you love them without words doesn't mean you shouldn't say the words. Tell that special person you love them every day. It's important for them to know, without a doubt, that you love them.

Actions and words – use them in conjunction.

WHEN HE'S UNSURE

If you go out on a date with a man, and when you sit down to get comfortable, you ask him what he looks for from woman, he stutters, "Uh, well, uh, see, I really, I...", that's your cue to get up and leave.

Go.

GO!

Yes, it's a drastic move, but your heart is worth it. See, the problem is, we think it's the people who play games that hurt us. It's not always the player who leaves the most painful scars. All it takes for somebody to hurt you is uncertainty about their own intentions, their own goals, their own morals, and their own motives.

If you're with someone who doesn't know who they are or what they want or what they stand for, I guarantee that you'll become collateral damage in their process of self-discovery.

So it's time to start asking questions. For starters, are you asking any questions at all? You can't get led on if you knew from the get-go where the relationship was going – or wasn't.

Start asking. Ask where this is going. Ask them where they want to lead you. Because if you want a man to lead you, you've gotta ask where he is going first. And if he doesn't know, then you've got to go.

FOOL'S GOLD

Fool's gold is called that because it actually looks like gold. It looks like the real thing, but it's worthless.

We see the same thing in our love lives sometimes. People spend their best years mining for gold, thinking they're getting rich as they fill up pail after pail after pail.

They're not really getting rich, they're just wasting time. It's not 'til they take it to the jeweler that they figure it out. What they've worked for all this time doesn't have any value.

Is that happening to us? Are we being fooled by fake people? Are we wasting years of our lives with people without authentic intentions, and it's not 'til we ask for a commitment that we figure out that they're not for real?

They were not for us. We've gotta start learning what's real and what's fake before we get taken in again. We've gotta started educating ourselves in this free space of singleness so we can learn how to discern people who have true intentions from those who don't.

If we don't, we're gonna waste more years of our lives thinking we're gonna retire off this big payday, we're gonna enjoy the payoffs of this relationship, only to find out when we ask this person to take it a step further, they have no intentions to be with us.

They weren't real in the first place.

Don't be a fool.

SHOW YOUR MATH

Now that I'm grown, I understand something.

You can say you love me in an emotional way, but I need you to show me that physically.

Yes, I get it. Love is an emotion. We know love by how we feel inside, but I need to see it through your actions, physically.

I need you to show your math. Remember in algebra class when your teacher said, "Okay, you got the right answers, but you didn't show your math, so you lost points"?

That's how it is in life. If you don't show your math when you say, "I love you," then I can't prove to myself that you really do. You can say you love me, but if you've got another person on the side, or you don't spend time with me, or you aren't attentive, or you don't put in the effort, or you don't communicate, then there's no way I can prove that you meant what you said. You aren't showing me that you know how to love in real life.

So, next the time you say you love me, I need you show me.

Show the math.

BE CAREFUL OF THOSE WHO FALL QUICK

Be careful about those who fall in love super, super fast, because they often fall out of it just as quickly.

Love can be used for so many different things. Think about it. It could be the most beautiful, the most horrible, the saddest, the happiest, the most exciting, the most depressing thing on earth.

It can be earth-shaking, earth-breaking, earth-bending, or earth-mending depending on whose hands it's in. Before you decide to give your heart to somebody, be sure their hands are prepared to carry that thing.

Love switches on people so fast. Don't be that bipolar love. Don't be that schizophrenic love. Be consistent. Be consistent, 'cause it can be all good this week and all bad next week. But you've gotta be unmovable in your faith and in your love and in your trust for a person.

WHERE ARE YOU GOING TO BE

The important question for relationships isn't, "Where are you?"

It's "Where are you going to be?"

More specifically, "Where are you going to be when things aren't as easy? When it's hard to love me right now? When decisions aren't as simple? When there's more on the line? Where are you going to be when the pressure is on in this relationship? Where are you going to be when you don't understand why I need you to follow me in something? You don't know where we're going, but I need you to follow me. Where are you going to be when money's tight? When situations come up? When sickness is here? Where am are you going to be?"

I think too often we are overly concerned about where the one we love is right now, as if this moment is going to last a lifetime. Sorry, it won't.

Things change. People change and circumstances change, but my love for you will never change. My place in your life will never change.

But I need to know if it's the same for you. Is it?

Because I don't care where you are right now. I'm more concerned about where you're going to be when I need you most.

YOU HAVE TO WORK

It's a fact that relationships where two people are perfect for each other can still fail. People often forget that you actually have to work at the relationship, even if you're a perfect match.

You have to work. They say that if you have a job you really love, you'll never work a day in your life. That's not true. Sure, it won't feel like work when you're with somebody you love. But that doesn't mean you don't have to work. There isn't an "easy button" for this. You can't skip the line.

You've gotta put in elbow grease. You've gotta put in time and attention. It's gonna feel like work sometimes, yes. But you've gotta be willing to do it. "I like you," is not good enough to sustain a relationship for 50 or 60 years.

But "I'm willing to work for you," is.

"I'm willing to work every day. We're in this relationship to make it work," is enough to get you there.

But are you willing to put that work in?

You may find the right person, but things between you will end in a breakup or worse if you're not willing to work for your relationship. Willy-nilly commitment doesn't work. Commit with your time and your energy and your ability to work.

QUIT BLAMING FACEBOOK

Facebook only makes it easier for people to be more of who they already were in the first place.

Facebook hasn't ever made somebody cheat. That person's heart did. Facebook isn't responsible for somebody being thirsty, their thirstiness is. Their habits are. Their desires are. Their eyes are. Their lack of discipline is the reason they cheated, not a social media site. Quit deflecting attention away from the core problem. People have to condition their hearts and minds to receive information without being tempted and acting on that temptation.

If that person can't handle a social media site, they can't handle your love. They're not strong enough to carry you. They're not dedicated and committed to integrity and faithfulness enough to be in a relationship with you.

Facebook is a website. Instagram is a website. Their heart is the reason they can't be in a relationship with you, not Facebook. Quit blaming Zuckerberg.

FACEBOOK

Facebook is getting everybody in trouble right now. With Messenger, you can see when that person has seen your message. In essence, I know that when I send you a message but you don't reply, we both know you did see it.

I'm not mad that you're busy. I'm actually happy that you have things to do. That's one of the reasons why I like you, you're responsible.

What I'm upset about is that when you see my message, you didn't think about taking two seconds out of your day to reply with a short, "Hey, how you been doing? I'm a little busy, can't talk right now." much less a thumbs up.

I'm not worth that. I'm not worth two seconds to you.

For anybody reading this, let me tell you something. If you're going through the same thing in life right now, it's not the fact that somebody is ignoring you that bothers you. It's that ignoring means. It means they can't take two seconds out of their day to say, "Hey, I'm a little busy. I appreciate you, so I'm going to get back at you soon."

Why should we give anyone our hearts if they can't give us two seconds?

IT RADIATES

You can't love another person until you first love yourself. It's not possible.

Let me tell you why. When you love yourself the right way, it radiates to everybody else. What you believe about yourself and how you feel about yourself radiate from inside you and to all of your relationships with others.

How?

Because when you love yourself right, you want to love other people. You want to share. You want to release the joy you have with other people. You want to help everybody else be happy – because you're happy with yourself just the way you are.

Conversely though, when you are unhappy, that feeling radiates from you and to everybody around you. To your relationships, your job, your friends, your family, everything.

I'm starting to think that maybe we've been taught to love wrong. We've been taught to love other people first, but not necessarily ourselves. We need to reverse the order and love ourselves first, then let that diffuse to everybody else we care about.

So no, I don't want you to love me more. I want you to love you more. Because if you love yourself the right way, you can love me the right way.

WOLVES IN KINGS' CLOTHING

You want to believe everybody in this world has true intentions. That everyone is good and pure at heart. But trust me, there are people walking around who are wolves in kings' clothing.

They're walking around pretending to be something they're not just to get something they want, from you. No matter how hard you try to deny that fact, no matter how deep you bury your head into the soil of ignorance, it doesn't change the fact that the person you're with is a wolf pretending to be a king.

Sometimes we lie to ourselves. We try to manufacture a belief that this person is something they clearly are not. We aide the wolves in their deceit. We've got to stop that. Right now.

I'm only telling you this truth because I love you. Every day I meet people out here who are getting bit by the wrong people disguised as the right people.

We need to be better about who we choose. It's only for so long that somebody can pretend to be something they not. Open your eyes. Trust your judgment when it counts. Use your senses to discover what lies beneath those royal garments.

PROTECT HER FROM YOU

What good is it to protect her from the whole wide world while her biggest fight is inside those four walls with you?

"Oh no, baby what are you doing?"

It's so easy to see when somebody else is treating your girl wrong. It's so easy to see the faults in other people and jump in front, yelling "Hold on, what are you doing, bro? Don't be like that!"

But are you that courageous when you are the one causing her hurt and being disrespectful? Are you looking at yourself in the mirror when you lash out? Are you ready to check yourself to make sure she's good? Is that really what you're doing? Or not?

Come on, I'm not trying to tell you how to run your life, but your house should be a safe haven. It should be the place where your lover can come home to be comfortable, unwind, and feel safe.

Safe from emotional, spiritual, and physical abuse. Her home should be her haven. Are you providing that?

Protecting her from the world is the easy part. The hard part is protecting her from our misguided desires, our personal shortcomings. Are you willing to do that?

UNCONDITIONAL

I'm going to love you unconditionally.

Which means I'm going to love you despite what the world may do to you, life may do to you, people may do to you – hell – even what you may do to you.

I'm going to love you unconditionally when life happens and you have no control. But you can control how you treat me.

But don't think my unconditional love means you can treat me bad. It doesn't. There's a clause in the contract of our relationship that says "Don't cover up the bullshit that you do to me."

You're supposed to love me. You're supposed to treat me right. Just because I'm your ride to die doesn't mean I will literally ride to die. I'm not going to die in this relationship. I'm going maintain how I feel about myself. I already love myself unconditionally. It's hard for me to love you unconditionally if that jeopardizes my love for me. It cancels it out. You can't do both.

Yes, I can love somebody unconditionally no matter what the circumstances are, but that don't mean I am unconditionally going to remain in a relationship, no matter what.

Those are two different things.

If you're going to love unconditionally, then love unconditionally.

If you can't, then we aren't meant to be, period.

ORDINARY

Never make the woman you care about – the one with super powers, the one who can fly, the one who jumps over buildings – feel ordinary. Like she's no different from any other woman. Early on in your relationship when she would open her inbox, she would see messages telling her, "You're beautiful."

So why does she go home to you now, but you don't even acknowledge that she looks nice today?

She still remembers getting dressed and going to the club with you. She remembers everybody stopping to look when she walked into the room, but she can't walk through the door of her house and get that same praise. Why don't you stop playing video games long enough for you to tell her she's beautiful in person?

She is the same woman you met. You just forgot how it felt the first time you went out, how nervous you were when you first introduced yourself to her, when you first inboxed her.

Never forget. Because there are men all over Facebook, Instagram, Snapchat, and Twitter, even at her office that she still makes nervous when she walks into a room or posts a picture.

Just because you don't feel nervous anymore doesn't mean she doesn't have super powers. The moment you begin to lose her – that is the moment when you'll decide to start treating her like she's extraordinarily amazing. I wish you treated her like it.

ANOTHER GIRL

When I find her, there will be certain things that I want to do for her all the time, like opening her doors, but I just won't be able to because I won't always be there.

I won't always be there to open your doors or buy you lunch or buy you dinner or fix you coffee or massage your feet. Sometimes I might be out of town. I might be doing something with work. But I can promise one thing – you will never have to worry about another girl.

When you're with me, you will never have to worry about another girl. When you care about somebody, you should never have to guess where their heart is. You will know every second, minute, hour that my heart is in your hands, always. I'm going to treat you special. You, not just any girl, but you. I'm going to give you complements when I'm around. I'm going to open your doors when I'm around. I'm going to fix you coffee when I'm around. I'm going to massage your feet when I'm around. I'm going to make you feel special when I'm around.

And you won't have to worry about another girl. I promise.

I CAN'T GIVE YOU

I hate to be the person who has to tell you this – but there isn't anybody on this earth, there isn't anything, and there is no force that can give you everything in life that you deserve.

How can I say that? Because you deserve so much more than can be quantified by human thinking. You matter more than space, time, and things that even no words can explain. You transcend everything that I can see or smell. You are royalty. In every sense of the word, you are God's child, so I can't give you what you deserve. You deserve the world and everything in it – and then some. The universe, the stars – I can't give you any of it.

But here's what I can give you.

The best of me.

That's it, that's all.

I'm hoping one day you will decide to take me up on that. In exchange, you'll receive my time, my effort, my faithfulness, my loyalty.

Maybe it doesn't matter that the person who loves you cannot give you everything that you deserve.

Maybe it doesn't matter.

MONDAY RELATIONSHIP

Is it Monday when you're reading this? If not, it soon will be – or it just was.

Nobody likes Mondays.

Unless you have a job you love, you hate having to go through the motions of getting yourself up and off to work.

The sad part about where I'm going with this is, most people have Mondays outside of work on different days of the week.

Are you in a relationship that's basically a Monday? A relationship where you dread having to stay in, always having to work out yet another problem?

Are you dreading the time you have to spend with that person? Do you wish you could put zero work into your relationship?

If any of that is the case, then you don't love your relationship as much as you should. You're not with the person you supposed to be with.

Because when you are with the person you're supposed to be with, you feel like you never have to work another day in your life.

So if you're sick of Monday, quit.

You should never dread Mondays.

Happy Monday.

NOT CHEAT BECAUSE OF YOU

Newsflash! Nobody in this world will ever be faithful because of you. They won't have integrity because of you. They won't not cheat because you do that one thing in the bed, that "little trick" of yours.

Nobody will ever not cheat because of that. They cheated or didn't cheat, were faithful or weren't, because of them. Because of who they are.

Too often we blame ourselves when things go wrong in a relationship, and we let it shatter our confidence because we think it's our fault.

No, it's everything wrong with them. You can't make somebody be faithful. If they don't wanna be faithful to themselves, if they don't fear letting themselves down, if they don't hold themselves to a high standard, if they don't love themselves...they can never love you.

How can a person love you for a lifetime and commit to you for a lifetime, if they haven't committed to themselves? I may sound crazy, but it's my belief that you gotta be with a person who fears disappointing themselves more than they fear disappointing you. That has to go for you too. That's how relationships work, and that's how they last.

WHY PEOPLE CHEAT

Remember back in school when you used to sit next to that person who used to always cheat on tests? No matter what, they'd ask you, "Hey, what did you get for number four? What's number four?"

Did you ever think to yourself, "Damn. Why are they always trying to cheat?"

It's because they weren't prepared for the test. They never took the time to study, to ready themselves for what was about to happen.

After you realize that, you didn't have to question why they're trying to cheat, because you knew. They're unprepared for the test.

You didn't blame yourself. You no longer asked yourself, "Why are they cheating?"

So why do you do the exact opposite in relationships? When somebody cheats on you, why do you take the blame and not fault them?

Your partner was the one who didn't prepare to handle themselves properly when the relationship went through a test. Every relationship is going to be tested. That doesn't mean you've got to cheat!

So when people cheat on you, understand that it has nothing to do with you and everything to do with them not being prepared for the tests that relationships bring.

NO PROOF NEEDED

There's something people need to stop doing.

Stop trying to prove somebody is cheating on you. Stop trying to prove somebody is doing wrong by you.

Stop trying to get actual physical proof, like you've gotta catch somebody in the act.

So you think that's your job. That's when you take off that crown, and you put on that detective hat. You start snooping. You go through phones, texts, Facebook messages, and emails.

You start texting people and making accusations, "Hey, woman to woman here. Are you messing with Jamal?"

You think it's your job to prove that he's cheating before you can leave. If or when that feeling ever comes, it's time to leave. Your suspicion is enough. Trust your gut. God gave you this intuition for a reason. Women have a special intuition where they just know.

Remember, you don't have to prove that somebody is cheating or doing wrong by you. If you feel like you can't trust that person, you can leave.

It's never worth trading your crown for that detective hat.

RELATIONSHIP WITH MYSELF

We go together. We're tight.

But I'm tighter with myself. I go with myself. I was with myself first.

You've gotta understand that. We've only been together for a little bit, but I've been with myself this whole lifetime, since I was born.

I've gotta make sure I'm happy. My number one rule is that I don't do tit-for-tat's.

"Just because you cheated, I'm gonna go cheat on you. Just because you hurt me, I'm gonna hurt you."

That's a problem. This relationship really isn't about you, it's about me. I'm not going to lose respect for myself just so that I can stay with you. I'm not that person. I don't care because I'm gotta think about how I'm gonna view myself, how the most important person I'm in a relationship with feels – me.

If you want tit-for-tat, I'm out.

HOT STOVE

When your hand hits that hot stove, are you going to yank it away or keep it there, thinking it won't hurt you anymore?

Do you want love to work for you so much that you ignore warning signs that indicate you're with the wrong person?

You reason with yourself, "I'm getting older."

You keep your hand there. You say, "But I've got kids."

You keep your hand there. You think, "Who else is gonna love me?"

You keep your hand there.

You made mistakes in your past, so you don't think somebody is gonna help you carry that baggage. You keep your hand there, and it burns. That person keeps hurting you. You want this to work so bad that you ignore the pain, and it starts to numb.

That's when it really hurts – you can't feel it anymore. Your heart decays on the inside. Now, you don't even want to love anymore. You've burnt away your desire to have true love by holding onto the wrong person for too long.

Don't ignore those warning signs. When you touch that stove and it burns you, leave.

WE BEEN THROUGH EVERYTHING

When couples say, "We been through everything, and we're still together," I can't believe it.

If you've been through everything, tell me why you haven't treated each other better. You should have to go through everything.

Maybe I just measure relationships differently. I want to look at how many milestones we've hit, not how many disasters we put each other through and survived.

Don't get me wrong. Being able to make it through the bad times is a good thing – unless that's the only good thing your relationship has.

Do you really wanna look back at your years together and say nothing but "We been through"?

"We been through a lotta fights...We been through the breakups...We been through you stepping out..."

You can have all the "We been through's" that you like if you want to. Not me.

NUMB ENOUGH

Maybe you're not numb enough just yet.

When you go to the dentist and they've gotta take a tooth out, what do they do first? They numb you up.

Why do they numb you up? It hurts! But that tooth has gotta come out because it's decaying. It's causing you problems, just like relationships do when things go wrong.

Sometimes, the only way to a healthy love life is to extract that person from your life like a decayed tooth.

But every time you try, you can't because it hurts. The thought of leaving hurts. The thought of being without that person hurts. But you know it's better for you in the long run if they are long-gone.

You keep pulling. You keep trying to get them out of your life, but you can't 'cause you can't stomach the pain. Sometimes it hurts too much to leave.

I understand that 'cause I've been there. But I'm here to tell you that it's only because you aren't numb enough yet.

At some point in this relationship, they will try to cause you pain, but you'll find yourself numbed.

When that numbness comes, the next step is to extract that person from your life.

Don't be numb and stay in this painful relationship just because you don't feel the hurt anymore.

A decaying tooth is still decaying whether you feel the pain or not.

WAIT ON YOU?

It's always those people who aren't sure about what they want in a relationship who expect you to wait for them.

But for what? What am I waiting for? You don't know what you want, so why should I even stick around?

If you are uncertain about us and me, then there are certain decisions I can't make for you. Some things I just don't need. On the top of that list is waiting for you. I can't wait around for you to decide whether or not I'm the person you want to spend the rest of your life with. I just can't do it because you might figure out I'm not that person. That means I'll have waited for nothing and missed other opportunities.

But it's not that I don't love you, because I do. It's just that I'm unwilling to love on your timetable. My heart is not a convenient scale for you. If you want me, want me right now. If not, I got to let you go.

That doesn't mean I can't come back. For right now, I've got to do me, and you've got to do you.

I'MA

Isn't it funny that when you get fed up with the drama and are ready to move on with your life, people throw their "I'mas" at you?

"I'ma start treating you better, I'ma starting doing right by you, I'ma be the man you need. I'ma, I'ma, I'ma..."

They always throw the I'ma instead of actually being there. Instead of actually doing better, they say "I'ma be better." Instead of actually being the person you need, they say "I'ma be the person you need."

These lies feed on your need to believe that people can and will be better and do better. The problem is, I'mas don't actually lead to people being better. That's when people get hurt. The actions never match the words.

We fall in love with people's potential, or what they say they're gonna do...instead of what they actually do.

Watch their actions. If they cared about you and wanted to treat you right, they would be doing it right now, not saying it. True love isn't about saying the right things, it's about doing the right things. So let "I'ma" leave their vocabulary for good. Stop accepting in exchange for your love. "I'ma" is not enough for you. Actually doing the right thing is.

WHEN SOMETHING BREAKS

When something breaks, three types of people are going to try and fix it.

You've got people who are actually gonna fix it.

You've got people who are gonna leave it the way it is.

And you've got people who sit around wondering why it broke in the first place.

Which one are you?

Are you the fixer? Are you the person who identifies something that's broken and realizes, "Oh, this has value. I want this in my life. I can't replace it, so I need to fix it. I need to work hard and make sure it's right."

Or are you the leaver? Are you the person who says, "Hey, it broke. I enjoyed it while I had it, but I'm ready to move on to something else. This is not what I want anymore."

I believe that either way, whether you're a fixer or a leaver, you're making progress.

It's the people who wonder why that I hate. They spend all their time wondering why something broke. Spending your time wasting your time. How much sense does that make? "Why" doesn't matter. It's broke, either fix it or leave it. Don't stay in a relationship purgatory wondering why something is no longer the way it was.

Hey, the shit broke. Do something about it. Don't be there because you can't figure out why it's broke. Don't be that person.

Fix it. Or leave it.

FACTS

Let me tell you what you're not gonna do.

When you cheat on me, abuse me, or break your promises to me, you're not gonna bring up, when I challenge you, how much you love me.

Right now, we are talking about this thing called a fact. The fact is, you cheated. That's something we can prove. There is a sequence of events. There are text messages. There's your confession that you cheated. That is an actual thing that happened – we both agree on the facts.

Your love for me is an opinion, and right now, I don't feel like discussing things that are subjective, that we differ on. 'Cause obviously, if you loved me the way you say you do, you would've loved me instead of cheating on me, hitting me, and abusing me.

But you did all those things, so those opinions we can save 'til later. Right, now we are talking about facts. So I'm not gonna waste my time talking about your opinion of love. You broke that promise to me, and that's what I'm concerned about.

We're talking about facts. So bring up facts, not opinions. Your love, after you cheat, is an opinion. It's no longer a fact to me.

TRAPPED

Do you feel like you're trapped? Like you don't know what to do? You don't know how to get out of the situation, so you just stay with this person? Why do you do that to yourself?

We both know you keep making excuses to give yourself a reason to stay. But your excuses are for them, not for yourself. You reason that you don't want to hurt them. But is the truth that you don't want to hurt yourself by going through a breakup? And you keep hoping that one day they're gonna leave you to make it easy, and then you'll be happy again – as if you can put your happiness in the hands of somebody else. Why are you putting the ball in their court? It ain't going anywhere!

You have to understand something. When you change, that change sometimes hurts other people. That may mean you have to get out of relationships you just don't want to be in anymore. It's gonna hurt. But it's necessary.

Here's why. Every step you take in the wrong direction with him is a step away from the right destination. Your happiness, where you are supposed to be, moves further and further away from you.

Come on. Take back that control. It's so easy to give it to other people. Don't.

If you don't want to be in that relationship, leave. Don't make excuses. Turn around, and walk in the right direction.

Towards your happiness.

REMEMBER EVERYTHING

Don't you hate it when you're minding your own business, enjoying your life, and all of a sudden your phone vibrates.

"Who is this?"

It's your ex.

And then he starts to take your emotions for a ride, "Hey, I was just thinking about you so I decided to text you, you know? Remember that time we went to that hotel and I bought you those flowers and that candy, and I... Remember when... Remember when..."

The crazy part about this is, every time an ex wants back into your life they always want you to "remember when".

So tell him.

"Yeah, I do. I remember when you used to hurt me. I remember when you left me hanging. I remember when you used to make me..." Tell him, "Yeah, I remember those good times too. The difference between me and you though, is that I remember everything, not just the select things."

So remember, exes got exed out of your life for a reason. But you won't remember that if you keep remembering only the good things but neglect to remember everything.

WHEN THEY LOVE YOU

When somebody loves you, there are certain things that they will not do to you. Love simply won't allow them to do it.

When they say, "I love you," and they really, really mean it, they won't cheat on you.

When they say, "I love you," and they really, really mean it, they won't abuse you.

When they say, "I love you," and they really, really mean it, they won't make you cry. They won't bring pain to the relationship. They won't bring stubbornness and pride when they really, really love you.

Love conditions the heart to be fond of the other person. Love always wants to see you do better.

Anybody can say, "I love you." But not everybody can live up to the expectations that professed love brings with it.

When somebody loves you, you don't need to tell them not to cheat. Love is always faithful.

WHO THEY WERE BEFORE

After the dust is settled and people have gotten comfortable in their relationship, they always revert to who they were before they met you.

When you met that person, there were a couple factors that influenced your perception of them. I'm damn sure one of them was lust. And then there's the fact that your partner has been on their very best behavior, heightening their form of themselves. They are who they think they need to be to impress you.

But once you get comfortable in this relationship, after six or seven months, the lust wears off, and that person's ability to keep that mask on to impress you starts to wear down, too.

Now, you think they've changed. But really, they've just reverted into the person they were before they met you.

Now you think you've gotta work on your relationship, 'cause you remember when it used to work easily. But it never really did work all that well, because you weren't in a relationship with that person, you were in a relationship with lust and with who they portrayed themselves to be.

Don't feel bad for walking away from a relationship in which a person has changed back into who they were before they met you.

They lied.

A DOG'S A DOG

Pop quiz!

What's a four-legged creature that wags its tail, sticks its tongue out, has canine teeth, and barks?

If you answered, "Dog," you are correct!

Okay, bonus extra credit now.

Would calling it, "Cat," turn the animal into something different? Would that make it not bark, or not have four legs, or not wag its tail, or not slobber over everything?

No. Calling it a dog, "Cat," wouldn't change anything about it.

We assign a title to something when it exhibits the characteristics that the title describes, not the other way around. You can't call a dog, "Cat," and expect it to meow, purr, and drink milk.

You also can't call a man, "Boyfriend," and then expect him to magically turn into somebody who exhibits the qualities of a good boyfriend. Just like calling a dog, "Cat," doesn't turn that dog into a cat, calling somebody your boyfriend doesn't necessarily make them worthy of the title.

Be careful. Don't get stuck with a dog.

YOUR POWER

Maybe he never learns because you never leave. It's a dangerous place to be when a person figures out you don't have the power to do what you've gotta do for you.

Think about the cycle. They do something, you take them back. They do something, you take them back again and again and again and again. Every time you do that, you reinforce their behavior as okay. You're out there believing you're generous to give second chances and third chances, but actually, you're giving the perpetrator more opportunities to perpetrate more deceit, more lies, and more mistrust.

You've got to start learning that nobody should get that comfortable, that nobody should think that they can do whatever they want to you. You can only control you, and your biggest asset in this relationship is your ability to leave.

I bet he would learn then.

How many times have you broken up with somebody, then that somebody magically changed? Somebody wants to do better now because you're gone. They know that if you have the power to leave, then they have to treat you the way you need to be treated. They have to respect you. They have to end the cycle themselves. Don't let anybody get so comfortable with you that they never think you could leave.

Because you can. That power is yours.

Don't let them take it.

FRIENDS AFTERWARDS

Stop thinking you can be friends with anybody. Because you can't.

Especially not with people you break up with.

Seriously, you just broke up nine hours ago and now you're agreeing to be friends?

Don't do it. If that 'ship is sinking, get as far away from that wreck as possible, or else you'll get pulled back in and go down for good.

Maybe you can have the "Can will still be friends talk" someday. But today isn't that day – not until you're completely over that person.

If I'm getting out of a relationship, I have to prepare my heart for life without you. How can I do that if we're still kicking it, talking, and acting like nothing changed? Then things won't actually change, and I'll be right back there.

To the people who still want to be friends with you, tell them your reason isn't that you don't love them. Your reason for turning down the friendship offer is that you love yourself more. You have to make progress. It's time for you to move on.

I'm not saying you can't ever be friends, but be friends with somebody when your heart is ready to accept the person is a friend – and only a friend. Nothing more.

LET IT HURT

One of the biggest hindrances we have as people is self-inflicted.

When we don't allow things to hurt us that should, we push ourselves further into a downward spiral that's harder and harder to get out of.

That heartbreak you're experiencing, are you actually letting it hurt you?

Sometimes you have to let your heart break completely before you to learn your lesson.

I see the opposite time and time again. What do we do instead of letting our hearts heal on their own schedule? We look for vices.

Instead of letting that heartbreak sit in our souls so we can grow from it, we mask it. We hide it. We pretend we're not hurt. We find another relationship to fill that void. We turn to alcohol or clubs or we hang with the wrong people.

Anything to mask the fact we were hurt. But we should let it hurt. Because if we do, we can grow – in the right direction.

Instead of filling our lives with bad habits and furthering our problems by being with the wrong people at the wrong time in our lives, let it hurt. Then you can grow.

And then you can heal.

MOVE TO THE NEXT

You're Goldilocks, and you're walking through a forest.
As you walk along, you see a lone cabin, and you go inside. You see some porridge.
Then you try it. "Oh, this porridge, it's too hot."
So don't eat anymore!
Sometimes, in relationships, people are too hot for you. Sometimes, that man is too aggressive. Too much brawn, too much alpha, too much dominance. Too much for you.
Move to the next bowl. Sit down at the next bowl, and take a bite. Your teeth start to shiver, 'cause it's too cold.
That man is too weak for you, too submissive, too sensitive. That bowl ain't the right one for you.
Move to the next bowl. This one is just right.
Let me tell you something – like that bowl, there's a person out there who is just right for you. Not too strong, not too weak. Just right. But you have to be cautious and confident enough to try the next bowl. It may be the right one, it may not.
Just keep moving until you find the right bowl.
It's out there. Trust me, Goldie.
And so is the relationship.

IT'S SUPPOSED TO HURT

There's no fast forward button for a broken heart. There's no magical fix, just time. Patience will help you get over the pain, but you can't get over it for good.

"I miss him."

You're supposed to. Breakups are supposed to hurt. You're a good person. Good people are supposed to feel something.

What are you going to do?

Seriously, are you going to let that loneliness make you love the wrong person again? Is that going to make you run back?

The only thing that can heal you right now is time. If you can battle through the loneliness and pain, you will get over the hill and find yourself beautiful.

That's not the answer people want to hear, but there's no easy button to it. When your heart is broken, it shatters. It takes time to put all of those pieces back together. That's the tough answer, but it's the right one.

You made the decision to break up with that person, so it was the right decision. You've got to stay on course, keep the faith, and go forward. Don't go backwards. That's how you lose, period.

GOOD MEN

Ladies, there are good men all around you, but you just don't think to look. You've been conditioned to think that they don't exist.

"I've been hurt before. Every man isn't trustworthy, every man is..." whatever.

Do you mean to tell me that one or two bad experiences are going to make you neglect the other 3.5 billion men out there? Other men are out there handling their business, moving up in their jobs, and taking care of their families. With everybody else out there, how can you possibly think that there's not somebody out there like that for you?

Look, I know there are times when you think about giving up because everybody you meet seems to let you down. But the only time you lose at this thing called love is when you give up on finding your Prince Charming, your partner in life because two or three jokers convinced you that good men don't exist or can't exist.

You need to convince yourself otherwise. Talk yourself into finding that right person for you. Then, maybe you will.

GOOD MEN (PT. 2)

You say good men don't exist. But they do.

"So where are they at then, Ace? Where are they at?"

First off, stop letting those few negative experiences hold so much power over our life. So those few people you've dealt with were bad men. Do you really want to let them speak on behalf of every man alive on this planet right now?

The residual relationship effect happens when you're not even with somebody anymore, but they affect every relationship you have going forward because you haven't properly healed.

Every time you think of a man, you think of that man who hurt you. You stayed in that relationship so long and you got hurt so much that you can't even fathom a good man existing because every time you see a man, you see him. You think about how he cheated, how he lied. You assume that everybody else would do the same. No, they won't.

Don't let those negative experiences determine your future love life. This time, close it out. Speak positive vibes only. See the good men who do exist; they're all around you!

You just have to open your eyes. Let go of that past experience. Don't hold Mr. Right responsible for what Mr. Wrong did, or you'll never get to meet him.

BE YOU

We doubt ourselves, and I hate it.

We doubt how awesome we are when other people don't see what we see in ourselves.

When others don't see what we wish they did, we start to question ourselves, "Damn, am I awesome? Well am I?"

We start to let how other people perceive us to change how we perceive ourselves. Then we start to change. We tell ourselves, "I need to be like this other person so I can attract people I like."

So you start doing your hair differently, you start to walk and talk different, you start to wear different clothes, and you start to hang out in different places.

But you forget something: You can only be truly happy when you look in the mirror and recognize the person that you see.

It's you. You thought that changing what you look like would attract the right people? How in the world are you going to get the person who's right for you if you don't look, act, or talk like you?

The sad thing is, people make this mistake all the time. They find themselves in relationships knowing they can't maintain the pace of pretending to be something they are not.

So when you do revert to who you always were, your boyfriend or girlfriend thinks you changed! No, you just decided to stop pretending, but you've broken someone's heart in the process. So save yourself – and other people – some heartache. Just be you.

Being you is going to get the person for you, period.

NOT OURS ANYMORE FOR A REASON

Why is it that we want stuff we can't have?

And why do we want something we can't have only when somebody else picks it up and starts playing with?

Why didn't we want it when we had it?

Some readers will think they know where I'm going with this.

"Oh, he's gonna talk about how we want somebody but only when that somebody is in a committed relationship already."

That's not what I'm talking about.

Why do we want things from people we are with but we know they can't give it to us? We know they don't have that one "must have" quality. We know they can't give us the love we need. Why do we desire things from people we know they don't have?

You want to love that person, but deep down you know they're not the one for you.

So you let them go. But now you're starting to want them back because you see them on Facebook or Instagram looking happy with somebody else.

Learn your lesson. You left for a reason.

Remember that reason. Don't want somebody simply because somebody else wants them now.

CONTROL YOUR THUMBS

The first step to happiness is putting your phone down. Put it down. Just put it down.

At night, when you're in bed by yourself, you feel lonely. The best thing to do is to put your phone down and go to sleep. Don't text. Resist the urge to text that wrong person you know you have no business talking to.

If you're having a good day, and you see something on Facebook or Instagram, or somebody texts you some BS, avoid the conflict. Just put your phone down. Walk away. Don't reply, don't text back. Replying is the first step to unhappiness.

Resist the urge. You have the power in your fingers to do the right thing. Engaging with unproductive people will make unproductive times in your life worse.

So be you. Don't text. Walk away.

SECOND CHANCE

Sometimes happiness begins when you realize there's a difference between forgiving somebody and giving them a second chance. Those are two different things.

Somebody keeps saying sorry to you, but you keep confusing the two. You keep giving somebody a second chance just because they say, "Sorry."

Sorry doesn't earn a second chance. Sorry earns forgiveness, sure. You forgive somebody not because they deserve it, but because you don't want to carry that burden in your life. You don't want their mistake to be the reason your heart is weighed down, so you forgive them. You release that transgression, but no sorry can earn a second chance. The actions after a sorry – those are what will earn a second chance.

If you love me, and you really want to correct things between us, you will do what it takes to earn my second chance. I will not give you one.

Stop giving people second chances so freely because they turn into third, fourth, and fifth chances.

Second chances are only earned when somebody turns away from their mistake that caused you pain, and they correct their behavior.

"Sorry," doesn't count.

TAKE HER PLACE

Your heart will never be satisfied with getting "borrowed time love" from somebody else.

Too many hearts out there are chasing, lusting, wanting to be loved by somebody who don't belong to them. When the person you want is committed to somebody else, they'll tell you, "Oh, we're not happy. I'm not happy with him. I don't even know why I'm with her. I want to be with you."

I don't care what that person tells you. If they wanted to be with you, they would be with you. But guess where they're at?

Laying in somebody else's bed. And where are you at? You're wanting to take her place, wanting to take his place.

You just might get what you want, so be careful what you wish. You might take her place and go from the being woman he's cheating with, to being the woman he's cheating on.

Be careful what you wish for.

TIME HEALS?

Want to know what I hate?

When people say, "Hey, just give it time. Time will heal your broken heart. Time will heal your wounds. Time, time, time..."

No, it won't.

If I drop my heart on the floor and walk out of the room, lock the door, and don't come back for two years, what am I going to find when I return?

A still broken heart, right there on the floor where I left it. Do you know why? Because time itself doesn't heal anything.

It takes more than time to heal you. It takes patience. It takes effort. It takes attention. It takes care over time, that's how you heal things.

So many of us believe that just because you give things time, those things are supposed to heal.

That is exactly the problem. Because when people hurt you, what do they expect? They expect that all they have to do is give you time, and you'll get over it.

No. You have to mend your heart after a breakup by consciously putting in the effort, time, attention, and patience. Time itself doesn't heal a thing.

KNOW ROLES

Some people aren't going to like this, but I'm going to get it out there anyway.

You know that you girl you go to the club with? She is just supposed to be that girl you go to the club with, not the girl you tell your secrets to.

She isn't supposed to be your best friend. Just because you have fun together doesn't mean that she's your best friend.

The same goes for women. Take that man you're sleeping with – come on, I know you're doing it. Just because it's cold outside or you feel lonely doesn't mean you should make him your everything. Don't turn him into your boyfriend if he doesn't have the qualities you expect in one.

Don't confuse roles, that's all I'm trying to say. Don't turn a limited role someone plays into a substantial one that they shouldn't. That's how we get hurt. When we put expectations on people who are only supposed to play a minor role in our lives, we can't appreciate the roles they do play. We can't assume they want more – or that they can even handle more. Recognize people for who they are and what they are.

If you're supposed to be a hater in my life, be a hater. But you will never be my best friend. Period.

TOO MANY PEOPLE

Let me tell you about a cycle.

A cycle we have to stop.

It's the cycle of women who think the good men are gone, so they give up on love.

It happens over, and over, and over.

That means we've gotta do our part.

Gentlemen, it's okay to be a gentleman. It's okay to pull out her chair, to open her door. It's okay to walk closer to the street. It's okay to stand up when she walk into the room and wait 'til she sits down before you do. It's okay to pick up the check. It's okay to get out of your car, walk to her door, and ring the doorbell. It's okay to do that. It's okay to address her mother as "Ma'am".

This is what women need.

Because you know what women get instead that makes them give up on love?

Men text, "Yo, I'm outside. Send me a nude."

There's a cycle of women who give up on love because the men have given up treating them right. They're not interested in investing in a woman and getting to know her.

How can you blame a woman for being picky when we're not doing our part? If we aren't treating her like a lady, there's no reason she should treat us like a gentleman.

How can we expect her to be one when if we aren't treating her like one?

TRUE FORGIVENESS

Is forgiveness earned or just given?
Take a second to think about it.
While you're thinking about it, let me give my answer.
To me, forgiveness is earned. Earned by you and me.
The one who's been wronged and the one doing the wronging.
We both have to work for forgiveness to be achieved.

The thing is though, you can't expect me to forgive you in one day when it took you months to do the damage. It's gonna take some time, and you're gonna have to put in some work.

And so do I. It's my job to wake up every morning and decide to forgive you again and again.

Now, I'm not saying you hold your forgiveness from people, that you refuse to give it to somebody that has earned it, but you gotta forgive on your time schedule. Don't just say you forgave somebody. Remember, anybody can say they forgave you, that's why it looks so easy to outsiders. But true forgiveness is earned. Take all the time you need.

BRICKS AROUND YOUR HEART

I see you with those bricks, laying those bricks down around your heart to build up that wall.

You want a wall tall enough so nobody can get close enough to hurt you anymore. You've got that shovel in your hand. You're digging a trench for a moat to fill with alligators. That castle wall is gonna protect your heart because you don't wanna get hurt again.

Guess what? You might not be wounded again, but nobody will ever be able to get close enough to love you, to help you.

Instead of building walls around your heart after it's been broken, build bridges. Build a way for safety to come help you. Build a way for aid, for love. That's the only way you can fix that broken heart.

Isolating it doesn't fix it.

Protecting it doesn't fix it.

REALLY LOVE YOU

Somebody says they love us, but their actions prove otherwise. I hate that.

How can you say you love me but you hurt me?

How can you say you love me but you aren't making time for me?

How can you say you love me when you don't consider my needs, my desires, and what I want out of life?

No, I'm not having any of that.

We've gotta hold ourselves to the same expectations we hold others to.

When it comes to how we love ourselves, we say we love ourselves, but we don't spend time with ourselves. We've always gotta be around somebody else. We don't spend time in isolation, growing our love for ourselves through meditation, prayer, and dating ourselves.

We say we love ourselves, but we stay in relationships with people who hurt us. We hurt ourselves by staying in relationships with people who say they love us but don't show it.

So don't just say you love yourself. Love yourself with your actions. Just like you expect him or her to say that they love you and back it up with actions, do the same for yourself. Love yourself by treating yourself right.

NEVER STOP LOVING YOU

In this life, somebody you may have given your whole heart to – your mind, your soul, kids, years – they may stop loving you. You've got to deal with that. But whatever you do, never stop loving you. Hold on tight to that love. Embrace it. Let that get you through the hurt days, because hurt will come. When it does, you've got to heal yourself. If you don't, you might let that hurt influence you to hurt other people. Hurt people, hurt people.

As long as you don't heal your heart properly, you may be motivated to hurt somebody else. I don't care if it's the person you want to stay who decides to leave. You've got to let them go.

If you don't, you'll end up hurting you and them. And that next person you get into a relationship with – if you don't let go of your ex – you may end up hurting them, too.

Learn how to love you. Because even when other people stop loving you, you'll be able to let them go and hold on to you.

MASK

Do me a favor. Pretend that this page you're reading right now is a mirror. Seriously.

I've got some questions for you.

You know I think you're gorgeous. I think you're the most beautiful girl in the world. And I admire you, I look up to you.

But I need to know something.

Here lately something's been going on. You stand in front of me and you cry, but you straighten up. You put on a mask, walk outside, and pretend everything's okay. You tell people you're fine, that you're doing well, that things couldn't be any better.

So why don't you tell the truth? Why don't you look at me the same way you used to? You used to smile when you saw me. Now you don't.

Next time we meet, can we have a talk?

I just want you to love me again, like you used to.

Sincerely,

Your Mirror

TURN THE HANDLE

Is it possible that your happiness is closer than you think?
No matter how close it is, you still have to work toward it.
Move forward.

Take one step after another, even if that means walking away from somebody that's holding you back.

Are you confident enough in yourself and your purpose to do that? Discovering the happiness on the other side of that door means leaving behind that somebody who's not meant to be in your life. Can you do make that choice?

See, this is what holds us back too often. We hold on to the wrong people, people who keep us from our opportunities, who keep us away from our blessings, who keep us away from our happiness by filling that void with so much hurt and pain that we don't have enough room for sunshine.

Are you willing to clear your plate?
Are you willing to turn that handle?
Are you willing to take one step after another?

No matter how difficult the next day may seem after you've left that person who's been keeping you from finding yourself and being confident in yourself, it will be worth it.

Love yourself first. And keep walking forward.

THEY MUST LOVE THEM

The hardest thing in life and in love is this:

To accept the fact that maybe, just maybe, I am too concerned with you loving me, convincing you to fall in love that I never realized you haven't first fallen in love with yourself.

Too often, we want other people to shower us with love, but we neglect their need to shower and bathe themselves in their own self-love first. You cannot give what you do not have. How can a person love you truly if they haven't mastered loving themselves first?

We get too wrapped up in how we want to be treated. We want to be loved, we want to be taken out, shown nice things. And we want to take, take, take, not realizing that maybe, just maybe, this relationship is supposed to be two people who love themselves as much as they love each other. That's how they're able to give love to each other. I love you. But I have to love me first. You do, too.

QUESTIONS

When did you stop being enough for you?

When did you stop being pretty enough for you?

When did you stop being enough for you to be happy?

When did you start relying on other people to fill the void that only you can fill yourself?

When did you start believing that you need somebody to complete you, not compliment you?

When did you start believing that you can't be happy until that special somebody comes along? Why do you have to wait until then?

Why do you put off having a purpose until you find somebody? Why can't you have your purpose right now?

Why can't you wake up tomorrow and be the better you that you've always wanted to be?

Why aren't you enough for you?

Why aren't you enough motivation for you to be better?

Why isn't your smile what you want to see on your face the most?

Why do you want to give everything to everybody else but you?

AFRAID OF TIME

You can't be afraid to wait. When you're afraid of time, you compromise. You start to settle because you don't think you have enough time to find what you want. And your friends don't help.

They tell you what's easy to hear, "Nobody's perfect. Your expectations are too high."

No. They only say that because they believe in time. They believe there's an expiration date on when you can find the right person for you.

I don't believe that. What are a few more years of searching for a lifetime of happiness? If you end up with someone who is no good for you because you compromised, you'll waste so much more time, and you'll be back right where you started – alone and impatient.

Write down the 10 qualities you want from a partner on paper right now. Once you've gotten them written, ask yourself, "You don't think you can find those 10 qualities in 1 person?"

If you take your time and search for a person with those qualities, you can and you will find them.

But for right now, I get it. It's hard. You're getting older. All your friends are getting married. You're feeling left out, so you're thinking about dropping some of those qualities you expect. That's only because you still believe in time.

I don't. I believe that when two people truly love each other, and they're right for each other, that love lasts forever.

Eternity is worth the wait. Trust me.

LET IT GO

Whatever happened from this moment on back into time doesn't exist anymore. It's only as real as we make it in our heads. Memories are only as real as we allow them to be.

The weight of the baggage you're carrying right now is only as heavy as you want it to be. We do have a choice to drop every negative thing in our lives – every negative person, every negative experience, even every heartbreak.

We have a choice to drop it all right now, to lighten our loads, and to move forward. But what are you going to do? Are you going to keep harboring those bad experiences inside your mind so you can't move forward in life? Then you won't go forward.

Are you going to keep letting that past mistake put obstacles in front of your future? Are you going to keep giving your heartache the satisfaction of knowing that it's hindering you from finding your happiness, your peace? Are you really gonna do that? Are you gonna live in confinement within your past?

No. Break free of that bondage.

Move forward. The future is waiting.

IN YOUR FEELINGS

We live in a world where being "in your feelings" is such a bad thing. But then we turn around and wonder why so many men and women live without rings. It's like people get praised nowadays for being cold and heartless!

"Girl, I cut him off like this. That'll teach him." What?

Or a dude says to his buddies, "Well, I don't love really her. I mean, whatever." Come on man!

One thing's for sure – we've gotta bring our feelings back. What happened to the days when you could admit to somebody that you liked them? That you think they're pretty, they're gorgeous, and you want to take them out? It didn't used to be lame to say those things.

There once were days that, when you got hurt, you would actually talk to the person about it, discuss it, and resolve it. You didn't try to conceal anything. That doesn't make you more of a woman or more of a man.

For this world to spin right with people living happily ever after on it, we have to bring feeling back. Are you with me?

LOOKING IN THE WRONG PLACES

I don't care where you look.

I don't care what mountains you climb, what valleys you dive into, what parts of the ocean your explore, or what nooks and crannies of this earth you search, or what sand castles you bury your face in.

Because you will never, ever be able to find happiness looking anywhere else but in your heart. There are so many people on this earth getting hurt right now because they're looking in all the wrong places.

Women, don't bury yourself inside of a man, thinking he'll bring you happiness. It won't. You can't put yourself in the bed of another person and think that is what's gonna bring you sunshine. It starts with you – within you. Don't bury yourself into another person until you've buried yourself in your heart so deep that you've found your own sunshine there.

AFRAID

You want love. You want your sunshine. You want everything to go perfect.

50 years from now, you want to have had your happily ever after and then some, 'til death do you part. And then even death won't stop you because your love is so great.

Or is it? Maybe, just maybe, you haven't caught a glimpse of the sunshine you want because you are too afraid to experience it. You're not afraid of love, but you are afraid what it takes to attain love. You're afraid to say yes to that date. You're afraid to say yes to the man who doesn't look or talk like what you're used to.

Are you too afraid to say, "I love you"? Are you too afraid to be honest? Too afraid to be you and find the right person for you? Too afraid to try new things?

Look, you can't be afraid of love if you ever want to experience it. I know you've been hurt before, but you've gotta let that guard down. It's time to try new things. If you want love, don't be afraid to express it, or be afraid to be open, or be afraid to be honest.

Maybe then you can find your sunshine. But one thing's for sure – you've gotta be honest.

WHEN HE HAD YOU

If he didn't want you when he had you, don't fall for his moves now that you've moved on to find happiness elsewhere.

Now he wants to step his game up. Now he wants to love you the way he should have in the beginning.

See, that's the difference. When somebody loves you, they don't need that extra motivation of somebody else treating you well, somebody else wanting to take you out, and somebody else wanting to treat you like a princess in order to change. They do that because they love you, because they care about you, because they appreciate you in the first place. Know the difference between somebody who wants you, and somebody who just doesn't want to see you happy with somebody else.

There are people out here who don't want to see you happy with anybody else but them, but when they have you, they don't do the necessary things that keep you happy.

Beware of men and women who only care when somebody else does. They only want to shine when somebody does. Sure, now he wants to open your door for you because somebody else just did! No, expect him to step his game up at the very beginning. True love always appreciates you, not only when somebody else does.

PUNISHING NEW RELATIONSHIPS

So you met the perfect person. This person is right for you. You've found yourself in a relationship with that person.

But you can't trust them. They haven't done anything wrong to you though. They didn't do anything to give you a reason to not trust them, but you reason with yourself, "I've been hurt before. Because I've been hurt, I can't trust you."

How is that fair? How can you punish your new partner for crimes committed by the old one? How can you do that and expect your relationship to work out?

You've gotta recalibrate your heart before you get into a new relationship. The reason you can't trust this new person is not just because of your ex, it's because you didn't take the proper time to adjust your heart settings back to default. You're still set on the heart settings of that bad relationship. Your heart is not adjusted for that new person. Now, you're punishing them and acting like the new person is the old person. That will never work.

Remain single until you can love somebody for who they are. A new partner is not your ex, so don't treat them like they are.

A GOOD MAN VS. THE RIGHT MAN

"Good men don't exist. If they did, I would have met one by now."

That's not true. Out of all the people you have dealt with in your life, you know there have been good men you've met – that alone proves your statement false.

Maybe the reason you haven't found a good man, or you don't see a good man, is because you think that every good man that you do meet, you have to be romantically interested in. That isn't the case. Don't confuse a good man with the right man for you.

Understand, the right man for you should be hard to find. You don't find a 50 or 60 years of happiness in marriage just plucking a guy off the man tree. It's going to be difficult to find that man, but a good man – that 3rd grade teacher, that doctor who takes care of his siblings, that man who sells you cookies at Subway – do you mean to tell me that all of them are liars and cheaters, too?

All I'm saying is, maybe you think that good men don't exist because you only think about good men in a romantic sense. But when you think outside of that box, good men come in different shapes and sizes. There are good men who will be interested in you and good men who won't be interested in you, and vice versa. Good men are all around you. Surround yourself with more good men, regardless of romantic interest, and you will find your trust in men rebuilt again. Trust me – I'm a good man.

MIRROR

Stop letting people replace your mirror. Stop letting their perception of you be the reflection of you.

Because guess what?

Somebody's going to tell you that you're too big.

Somebody's going to tell you that you're not beautiful.

Somebody's going to tell you that your lips are too thin.

Somebody's going to tell you that your hair's not straight enough, or it's not long enough.

That you're too dark. That you're not light enough.

Somebody's going to tell you all these things in hopes of replacing your opinion of your with theirs.

But you've got two eyes for a reason. You have a mirror for a reason. So I want you wake up every day and say, "Ooh, look how stunning I look. Ooh, look how beautiful I am. Ooh, look at how much of a queen I am."

You're going to see that for yourself. And you're got to start believing that. That's the only thing that matters. Because you are given a mirror for a reason. There's a reason you have a mirror and two eyes. Start using it to formulate your own opinions about yourself and stick to them, no matter what somebody else says. The only thing that matters is your self-confidence. It's too valuable to be weighed down by everybody else. Stop letting them be your mirror. See yours.

ONE HEART

At birth, we are given things as we enter this world.

You were given ten toes, ten fingers, two lungs, two nostrils, a whole bunch of teeth, two eyes, and two ears to hear.

You were given all those things, but you were only given one heart. That means you've gotta take extra care of it. Not just anybody can hold that heart of yours because it's the most important you have. Although it's a strong muscle, when it breaks, it can affect your whole body. It can affect everything – every muscle, every fiber, every tendon, every toe, every hair. Your heart is your lifeline...to life itself.

So before you give your lifeline to somebody else, be sure that they are equipped to take care of it. Be sure that they know the in's and out's of it , that they'll never break it. Because once your heart breaks, that scar may never leave.

Be careful. You've only got one heart.

TRUST ONE PERSON

You've had your heart broken.
You're thinking about giving up on love.
Maybe you already have.
Not just given up on love with the person who broke your trust, but given up on the whole idea of love.
Let me tell you something. I'm not going to be one of those typical gurus who ask you to start trusting men again. I don't need you to start trusting and giving second changes to anybody and everybody, I need you to start trusting a single person, that one person who's out there for you. What's breaking your heart right now is the belief that all men are supposed to be right for you. That's not how it works.
If your heart's been broken one, two, three, ten, thirteen, fourteen times, that means you haven't found the right one person for you. I don't care if most people in the world are bad, because all you need is one person. Before you give up on love, remember that you don't have to trust people, you just have to trust your person, that one person you are going to meet someday.
Don't give up on love just yet.

BUT YOU

How do you believe in everybody else but you?

How do you trust everybody else but you?

How do you love him but not love you?

How do you trust them but not trust us?

How do you rely on everybody else's plan but yours?

Why do you think somebody has a better plan for your life than you do?

Why do you value their opinions more than you do yours?

When are you gonna start counting on yourself to make you happy?

When are you gonna start trusting your decisions?

When are you gonna let your feet guide you?

When are you gonna look for a partner in this thing called life and not rely on somebody to give you a life?

When are you gonna start trusting and loving you the way you trust and love everybody else?

TAKE A BREATH

Do me a favor.

I don't care who's looking.

I don't care if this makes you look odd or not.

Take a deep breath.

Then do it again.

Now I want you to remember something.

Remember that if you can do that, it's not that bad.

If you can take a deep breath right now, then your life is not as bad as you think.

Right now, you may be feeling discouraged. Or you may feel like things are not going your way, and you're not measuring up to the standards you want to hold yourself to.

But remember, no matter how bad it seems, you are still breathing.

There are people that didn't wake up this morning. There are people who took their last breath yesterday. But you are blessed to take another breath, so take a breath and count that blessing. Keep moving forward. Let that motivate you to keep going after your dreams.

Keep going after your success story, because it's there.

All you've got to do is breathe. Then you'll know that it's alright.

WOULD HAVE BEEN WORTH IT

When you finally walked your ass across that stage and got that piece of paper, it all became worth it, didn't it?

Think about all those sleepless nights. All those times you thought you were gonna flunk out of school. All those ramen noodle packets. All those negative, hateful-ass professors.

Everything became worth it because you didn't let anything stop you. You kept your head focused on your goal, and you finally achieved it. And it was worth it.

Now think about finding that right person. It's gonna take some sleepless nights. It's gonna take some times when you're gonna fail at relationships. You're gonna have to regroup, but you've gotta stay focused.

When you finally walk yourself down that aisle and get that ring, it will all have been worth it.

It will be worth it. Nothing in life that's worth having comes easy. You've gotta work for it. Stay focused. Don't let anybody distract you from your goal.

SOMEBODY WILL LOVE YOU

Somebody will love you.
Say it until you believe it.
Somebody will care for you.
Say it until you believe it.
It will happen. Understand, it's not gonna be easy. You might meet the wrong person first. That person you give your heart to – they may drop it, they damage it. Now you have baggage. Now you think nobody else will care for you. Nobody else will love you.

You're gonna start questioning yourself. You're gonna say, "I'm not as young as I used to be. My body doesn't look the same. I'm not the same person who can give. I'm guarded. Who's gonna want this?"

Yes, you're gonna question yourself because other people don't love you when they should.

But I need you to say, "Somebody's gonna love me," until you believe it. "Somebody's gonna care for me."

Then walk to your mirror and say it.

It's time to act in harmony with the words you've just said. Love yourself. Be the somebody who's gonna love you. Show your heart that it can be loved.

I promise that other people will follow your example. But you've gotta love you first.

GET OUT THERE

You know those people who read a hundred and one self-help books but never do anything about it? It's like they can read about helping themselves, but they never actually follow through and do.

Don't be like those people. Don't add this book to the list of books you've read…but never did anything about.

Every chapter in my book is a point of view, a strategy to deal with the good times and the bad times of relationships.

But they mean nothing if they're not applied. It's like love – you can tell me you love me, but I don't want you to if you're not gonna show it.

In the same way, don't read my book if you're not gonna apply it.

If you're in a negative relationship and you know it, everybody knows it, leave. Leave now. If I can help save just one person from getting their heart broken again, all the time I put into writing this book and getting it into people's hands will be worth it.

If you're in a positive relationship, keep the lines of communication open. Every day, commit to showing how much you love that person, and you'll see the next 50 to 60 years become your "happily ever after."

If you're single and looking to mingle, be careful. Know your standards, and watch your thumbs. If that man or woman doesn't prove they love you the way you love yourself, they don't deserve you. It's time to bounce.

Regardless of where you're at – and you know where you're at, or else you wouldn't be reading this – today is the day to make a change.

Today is the day you can start to change your life for the better for good by treating yourself better, by treating your partner with the respect and admiration you know they deserve.

Today is the day.

So get out there.

ABOUT ACE METAPHOR

This book was inspired by you, for you.

I am merely the vessel, the voice.

Therefore –

This book will remain to be not about me.

But rather,

About you.

www.acemetaphor.com